The Give-Away

A Christmas Story

Written and Illustrated by
Ray Buckley

Abingdon Press

Nashville

The Give-Away

Copyright © 1999 by Abingdon Press

Book design: R. E. Osborne

ISBN 0-687-07186-0

01 02 03 04 05 06 07 08 – 10 9 8 7 6 5 4 3

Printed in Hong Kong

For Rick

A note from the author

Among the Northern Plains tribes, all of creation (humanity, animals, bird, insects, and plants) are part of the sacred hoop. The Lakota expression is *mitakuye oyasin*, literally, "all my relations." It is an important theological concept that the birth of Jesus took place in a stable, to signify not just a lowly birth but also in the presence of the Four-Leggeds and Those Who Fly. The message of Jesus becomes one not only of restoring humanity to God, and human-to-human, but also of restoring humanity to "all our relations."

The artwork in *The Give-Away* reflects a variety of North American wildlife and plants. While not a story from Native traditions, the art includes designs inspired by various tribes. Among the Northern Plains tribes it was the custom to paint portions of the face red, as a symbol of hospitality and friendliness. The pictures of the animals in this story reflect that custom.

There was a grove of trees where the forest grew thick. The trees had stood there for as long as anyone could remember, their roots intertwined so that nothing could affect one without affecting them all. They were known to the inhabitants of the forest, the Four-Leggeds and Those Who Fly, as the Old Ones. In the middle of the Old Ones stood the oldest of them all, taller and broader than the others. If one stood beneath it, one could not see where its crown touched Father Sky, and smaller trees grew around its roots in the safety of its vastness. It was called the Ancient One, for it had known the Creator longest of all.

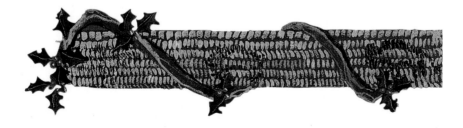

It was to this grove that the creatures of the forest and the plains, the Four-Leggeds and Those Who Fly, gathered for council. Each had sent one speaker, the oldest and the wisest of its kind. Snow fell thick on familiar paths, and each arrived in silence, waiting with the patience of those who have seen much. When the circle was complete, they stood listening to their hearts.

"They have lost their way," Whooping Crane said. "There is no pattern to their journey."

Snow Goose nodded in agreement.

"They have lost their purpose," Deer Mouse said softly. "They do not gather seeds. They do not know who they are."

9

Tatanka, the Bull Buffalo, dropped his head low.
"They take more than they need and give nothing back.
They do not give away."

"They do not see long-distance," Eagle began. "They keep more than they can eat, while some are hungry. They no longer know that they are connected."

11

"They do not know that they are beautiful," Fox said
sadly, her white coat blending with the snow. "They
decorate themselves with stones and hide their Spirits."

12

"They think that power is what they can hold on to," Old
Beaver pondered. "They say, 'This is mine,' and build lodges
too large so that they, themselves, will appear big."

"They must make others small, so that they will look big," Bear's deep voice answered. "In the end, they must destroy themselves or others. They have lost their names, and do not know who they are."

G randmother Turtle, who was the last to arrive, made her way slowly to the center of the council. She lifted her head so she could see all who gathered beneath the Old Ones. Her voice was barely audible. "We must give-away ourselves to them. We must speak to them in soft voices. We must remind them of who they are."

She paused, lowering her head into her shell. Then suddenly, she lifted her head as high as her neck would allow. "I will give them my shell," she said with certainty. "I will come with no protection, and they can use my shell to adorn themselves."

Around the circle, the council was silent. The Wind did not blow through the trees. Not a single branch on the Old Ones fluttered. The forest was still as Grandmother Turtle began her walk back to the empty spot in the circle.

"I will teach them the patterns of life," Whooping Crane said slowly. "Snow Goose and I will remind them of the seasons."

"I will teach them to gather seeds so that no one need be hungry," Deer Mouse began. "I will give them what I have stored."

Eagle searched the night sky and, without lowering her
head, said, "I will give them my feathers. Perhaps if I
cannot fly, they will not feel small."

20

Tatanka, the Bull Buffalo, stood with his legs squarely on the Earth. "I will give them my flesh to sustain them, and my skin to warm them. I will give myself away."

Each council member in turn rose to
speak of the gift, that most costly
portion of themselves, that each
would give away. When the circle was
complete, a new voice was heard. In
the shadow of the Ancient One
stood the Creator.

"Ho, children!" the Creator began softly. "You will give yourselves away, but they will not know that. They will say, 'See what I have taken!' and think that they have made themselves larger."

For a moment, the Creator paused. "It is I who must give myself away. I must give-away my protection and come vulnerable to their lodges. I must choose to become small, so that they can choose to know me large. I must give-away my Name, so that they can know their names."

The Ancient One had stood silent. The sound of his voice had not been heard in many winters. "Creator, how can this be? How can the Great Mystery become small?"

The Creator stood beneath the Ancient One. The shadow of the great tree became light, and the grove of the Old Ones became full of the presence of the Creator. "A baby will be born. He will be the Son of the Great Mystery. He will be born not where the Two-Leggeds are gathered, but among the Four-Leggeds and Those Who Fly. He will bring light into confusion. He will bring hope into despair. He will bring love, and his name will be great."

The Ancient One began to tremble, and Those Who Fly left its old branches. The grove of the Old Ones moved in its quake. "Creator, what can I, whose name speaks only of my age, give-away to the Great Mystery become baby? What can I do from my grove in the forest?"

The Creator turned toward the Ancient One. The voice of the Creator was low. "You will be his support. You will be his place of rest. You will hold his body. You will hold him up. In the beginning and the end."

And the Ancient One wept, partly for joy and partly for sorrow.